The Spiritual Gifts

*GOD'S PLAN FOR USING YOU
TO BUILD UP THE BODY OF CHRIST*

By Kris Van Hook

PART 1

ARE THE SPIRITUAL GIFTS FOR TODAY'S CHURCH?

Over the years, a controversy has brewed over spiritual gifts and whether they are legitimately operating in the church today. Some say that these gifts, or at least some of the gifts, are not available today and therefore any claim of their manifestation is illegitimate. Others disagree, saying all the gifts should operate today, just as they did during the early church period. So let's take a scriptural look at this topic because our understanding of this subject has great bearing on the life of the church.

Why is this an important topic for us to study? Is it essential for salvation? No, it's not, but it *is* extremely important in our personal relationship with the Lord, and certainly affects the work of the ministry that God has for each one of us. How we see and understand the gifts of the Spirit affects how we relate to each other and the world around us. It can dictate the type of ministry we have, so we need to have a firm grasp on what we believe about spiritual gifts.

Let's look at what Paul says in 1 Corinthians 12:1— *"Now about spiritual gifts, brothers, I do not want you to be ignorant"* (NIV). The word "gifts" is not actually in the original Greek text. It should read "about spirituals." It is possible that the word "gifts" is implied, but looking at the context, it seems likely that Paul was speaking about people, who were gifted but misusing the gifts. In either case, Paul will keep us from being ignorant concerning the gifts. The Greek word for "spiritual" comes from the root word "pneuma" and denotes its' divine origin.

Here is the Strong's definition for gifts: NT: 5486 charisma (khar'-is-mah); from NT: 5483; a (divine) gratuity, i.e. deliverance (from danger or passion); (specifically) a (spiritual) endowment, i.e. (subjectively) religious qualification, or (objectively) miraculous faculty.[1]

When you put this together, it is clear that these gifts have a divine origin.

So let's follow Paul's exhortation and jump into the scriptures with both feet to see what it says about this subject. To understand the teaching about spiritual gifts, we must ask ourselves some questions.

1. What are they?
2. By whom were they given?
3. When were they given?
4. Why were they given?

Question 1: What are they?

Let's start by looking at the passages that specifically describe these gifts. There are two lists given in the New Testament. The first in Romans 12:6-8— *"we have different gifts, according to the grace given us. If a man's gift is prophesying, let him use it in proportion to his faith. If it is serving, let him serve; if it is teaching, let him teach; if it is encouraging, let him encourage; if it is contributing to the needs of others, let him give generously; if it is leadership, let him govern diligently; if it is showing mercy, let him do it cheerfully"*(NIV).

The second list is found in 1 Corinthians 12:8-10-- *"To one there is given through the Spirit the message of wisdom, to another the message of knowledge by means of the same Spirit, to another faith by the same Spirit, to another gifts of healing by that one Spirit, to another miraculous powers, to another prophecy, to another distinguishing between spirits, to another speaking in different kinds of tongues, and to still another the interpretation of tongues"* (NIV).

Let's sum up this list:

1. Prophesy
2. Serving
3. Teaching
4. Encouraging or exhortation
5. Giving
6. Leadership
7. Mercy
8. Message of wisdom (utterance in ESV) (word of wisdom in NASU)
9. Message of knowledge
10. Faith
11. Healing
12. Miracles
13. Distinguishing between spirits
14. Various kinds of tongues
15. Interpretation of tongues

I will go into a little more detail on some of these gifts later on, but now that we have seen what they are, let's go ahead and answer the other questions we mentioned earlier.

Question 2: By whom were they given?

Look again at the 1 Corinthians passage. It seems very clear that the gifts are given specifically by the Holy Spirit. The apostle Paul left no doubt about the origin of spiritual gifts. Look down a little further to verses 11-13. One of the keys to understanding spiritual gifts is contained in verse 13. This speaks of the baptism, or infilling, of the Holy Spirit and its significance in terms of empowering us to do what God has for us to do.

You can see here that it is the Holy Spirit who bestows these gifts to believers. He can do that because He is God. Now, some people seem to have a hard time with the whole concept of the Holy Spirit being God. They would agree that the Bible teaches a triune God—Father, Son and Holy Spirit—but then seem to want to relegate the Spirit to second-class Godhood. Remember, the Holy Spirit *is* God! He has all the same attributes as the Father and Jesus the Son. He can do whatever He wills to do.

Perhaps it's possible that the reason some people have difficulty with this concept is because the Holy Spirit does not exalt Himself, but Jesus. But the Holy Spirit is just as much God as the Father and the Son and we should obey His instruction to us. Remember what Jesus said about the Holy Spirit in John 16:7-11:

"But I tell you the truth: It is for your good that I am going away. Unless I go away, the Counselor will not come to you; but if I go, I will send him to you. When he comes, he will convict the world of guilt in regard to sin and righteousness and judgment: in regard to sin, because men do not believe in me; in regard to righteousness, because I am going to the Father, where you can see me no longer; and in regard to judgment, because the prince of this world now stands condemned"(NIV).

Even Jesus relied on the power of the Holy Spirit while He was here in human form. Remember that Jesus set aside some of His divine attributes while He was on earth (Philippians 2:6-7). He was in perfect relationship with the Father and the Spirit, relying on the Holy Spirit to help Him accomplish the mission set before Him by the Father.

The work of the Holy Spirit is so important that Jesus said in Matthew 12:31 that anyone who speaks a word against the Son of Man will be forgiven, but one who speaks against the Holy Spirit will not be forgiven. As you can see then, our belief about the person of the Holy Spirit is vital. When Jesus taught about being born again, He said that our second birth is the birth of the Spirit into our lives and that the Spirit would teach us, guide us, comfort us, and empower us. If you want to look at some of the scriptures concerning this, you can look at Matthew 28:19; Mark 3:16, 13:11; Luke 11:13, 12:12; John 3:5-6, 7:39, 16:13-15.

Question 3: When were they given?

Read Acts 2:1-5. No legitimate biblical scholar disagrees that this day of Pentecost (50 days after the feast of First Fruits) was the first indication that the Holy Spirit began imparting the spiritual gifts to the fledgling church. In fact, most would say that this day is the very birth of the church. Peter explains what took place in verses 17-20 and indicates that this began the period of the "last days." These first gifts were imparted as the believers were filled with the Spirit and verse 4 says *"as the Spirit enabled them."* That phrase is critical to our understanding of spiritual gifts.

Question 4: Why were they given?

Let's go back to Romans 12 and start in verse 1 (through 5). Notice that Paul connects the list of gifts to his teaching about offering our bodies as living sacrifices and being connected together as one body. In the First Corinthians passage, he says this–*"But to each one is given the manifestation of the Spirit for the common good"* (12:7). He goes on in the rest of the chapter to explain that this is all a part of being able to work together as one body and that not all have the same gifts. This was done intentionally, so that we would be interdependent on one another. This destroys the concept held by some that you can be a "lone ranger Christian," and do not need to fellowship on a regular basis with a body of believers. God purposely gave us each different gifts to keep us in need of one another to fulfill His purpose for the church.

Why the controversy?

To tell you the truth, I don't completely understand why there is so much controversy. I think Scripture is rather clear on the subject, but I'll make an attempt at an explanation. There isn't much disagreement about spiritual gifts being in operation in the church today. The question is whether or not *all* of these gifts operating legitimately, and are all of them necessary in the church today?

There are Bible teachers whom I respect greatly, who teach that some of these gifts are natural and some are supernatural. Look at the list again and you can probably recognize which ones they are putting in the supernatural category. Prophesy, utterance of knowledge, utterance of wisdom, healing, miracles, distinguishing of spirits, and most especially, tongues. They might also use the term "miraculous" for these particular gifts.

These teachers usually claim that these gifts stopped when the canon of Scripture was completed. The reasoning used, is that those gifts are not necessary anymore because we have the revealed Word of God to use, rather than relying on those gifts. The verse most often quoted to defend that position is in 1 Corinthians— *"Love never ends. As for prophecies, they will pass away; as for tongues, they will cease; as for knowledge, it will pass away. For we know in part and we prophesy in part, but when the perfect comes, the partial will pass away"* (13:8-10, ESV).

Clearly, the passage does mention three gifts as examples of gifts that will pass away, but in order to make that passage work, "the perfect" has to be the Bible, and "in part" or "partial" must represent those supernatural gifts.

Though that is a possibility, it certainly could be considered a stretch. There is room for debate about what this verse means and one proof text is not sufficient to "hang your hat on." Many Bible commentators lean toward the "perfect" referring to that state of being in heaven or the presence of the Lord. Here are some examples:

"[But when that which is perfect is come] Does come; or shall come. This proposition is couched in a general form. It means that when anything which is perfect is seen or enjoyed, then that which is imperfect is forgotten, laid aside, or vanishes. Thus, in the full and perfect light of day, the imperfect and feeble light of the stars vanishes. The sense here is that "in heaven" - a state of absolute perfection-that which is "in part," or which is imperfect, shall be lost in superior brightness. All imperfection will vanish. And all that we here possess that is obscure shall be lost in the superior and perfect glory of that eternal world. All our present unsatisfactory modes of obtaining knowledge shall be unknown. All shall be clear, bright, and eternal." [2]

"[But when that which is perfect] the state of eternal blessedness; then that which is in part-that which is imperfect, shall be done away; the imperfect as well as the probationary state shall cease forever." "A few have suggested that this state of perfection will not be reached until the new heavens and new earth are established. Another point of view understands perfection to describe the state of the church when God's program for it is consummated at the coming of Christ. There is much to commend this view, including the natural accord it enjoys with the illustration of growth and maturity which Paul used in the following verses." The often-quoted Greek scholar, Kittle, says this: "In the Pauline corpus the meaning "whole" is suggested at 1 Corinthians 13:10 by the antithesis to Spiritual gifts — Tongues, knowledge and prophecy are mentioned— do not give full knowledge of God. This will be granted to the Christian only with the immediacy of face-to-face," [3]

Verse 12 of this same passage seems to support the idea that the "perfect" is when we are face to face with Jesus: *For now we see in a mirror dimly, but then face to face. Now I know in part; then I shall know fully, even as I have been fully known"* (1 Cor 13:12, ESV). I think it's obvious that when we are face to face with Jesus Himself, we will no longer need *any* of the spiritual gifts.

Let's ask another question. As you look back at the lists given in Romans and 1 Corinthians, keeping in context with the verses surrounding them, do you see Paul making any distinction as to the *nature* of these gifts? Does He give any indication that any of these gifts are natural? I would have to say no!

The fact that the Holy Spirit imparts these gifts makes every single one of them supernatural. We have nothing in our natural state that is valuable for the spiritual growth of ourselves or anybody else. The only thing of spiritual value we have is that which God has bestowed upon us. Therefore there cannot be two categories of spiritual gifts, but only one. They are unmerited gifts of grace, given to us by the

Holy Spirit. Now, Paul did say that we are to desire the *greater* gifts (v. 31) and that even more excellent than this was *love*. But it's interesting to look at which gifts Paul considered greater.

"Pursue love, yet desire earnestly spiritual gifts, but especially that you may prophesy" (1 Cor 14:1). He goes on to explain why, and yet still says he wishes all spoke in tongues. He also seems to indicate that *interpretation* is greater because of its value to the body. Let's ask some more questions.

If some of these gifts were going to pass away after just some sixty to one hundred years (after the New Testament Scripture was completed), why would Paul spend so much time instructing the church about their use? Yes, he was correcting the Corinthians in the misuse of the gifts, but in so doing he was giving instructions to the whole body of Christ. Why did Paul make no other distinction of the gifts? Why did he say to earnestly desire all of these gifts?

Are these gifts really unnecessary today because we have the canon of Scripture? Why then would the verses about these gifts be included *in* the canon of Scripture? Why would Paul tell the church in Thessalonica not to despise prophecies, but instead test them and hold fast to what is good? (1Thes 5:20). Was that just for them and not later believers?

With all this evidence, what is it that makes people want to dismiss certain gifts and claim that they have already passed away? Is it biblical evidence or something else? Let me throw out a couple of reasons. You are welcome to throw them right back at me if you disagree. I believe there are two different categories of churches or teachers in this camp.

In one group are the churches that don't believe in miracles at all, and certainly don't give the working of the Holy Spirit any credibility. Many old mainline denominations have gone this direction. They've been influenced over the years by a movement called "higher criticism," a form of "Bible study" that tried to explain the Bible through secular means, which automatically discounted miracles and the supernatural. Thus, if they couldn't explain an event in the

Bible by means of science, they determined it must not be accurate and looked for some other explanation.

As an example, they would explain the miracle of God parting the Red Sea for the nation of Israel to cross over this way: "Well, actually the Red Sea was really the "Reed Sea" and it was only a few inches deep. No miracle here." Really? How interesting that Pharaoh's army all drowned in a few inches of water! [4]

This approach to God's Word has led to the destruction of many denominations that used to be evangelical. Their seminaries deny the basic doctrines of the Bible. Creation (they prefer evolution), the worldwide flood, the virgin birth, the miracles of Jesus, some even deny the Resurrection. They have a low view of the Bible and do not believe in its inerrancy. So it stands to reason that they would not accept supernatural gifts of the Holy Spirit. Is it any wonder that the attendance in many of these churches has fallen significantly? [5]

The second group is, at least from my perspective, harder to understand. These are the churches and teachers who vigorously defend the inerrancy and infallibility of the Bible and study it thoroughly. Looking at the scriptures as we have makes me wonder. Why do they come to the conclusion that certain gifts are not available today? Again, is it really from their study of the scriptures concerning this subject, or is it something else?

There is one other reason I can think of. I believe it's possible that seeing the misuse, abuse, and even some ridiculous fraud concerning these gifts, they throw the baby out with the bathwater. They don't want to be associated with this abuse and so they may look at the scriptures with a slightly prejudiced view. I completely understand that. I detest some of the things that go on in the name of the Holy Spirit and I know that the Lord must be grieved as well.

It is not, however, necessary to disregard some gifts because people abuse them. Generally, it's fairly easy to tell the fraudulent appearance of these gifts. Start by looking at who is being exalted. Is it God or man? If it's man, there's a problem. Then, do as the apostle John suggested in 1 John 4:1-3— " *Beloved, do not believe every spirit, but test the spirits to see whether they are from God, because many false prophets have gone out into the world. By this you know the Spirit of God: every spirit that confesses that Jesus Christ has come in the flesh is from God; and every spirit that does not confess Jesus is not from God; this is the spirit of the antichrist."*

If a prophecy turns out to not be true, do not listen to the so-called prophet. If a word of knowledge is inaccurate, it is not from God but man. If tongues are not used according to Paul's order in church, then follow his instruction to be silent. But we must stay on course with what the Bible teaches about this, and I believe we have seen no biblical evidence to categorize these gifts differently and say that some do not exist anymore.

I've actually heard people misspeak about 2 Peter 1:3, saying that the *Bible* has all we need for life and godliness, to prove that we don't need these gifts. Let's look at it—*"seeing that His divine power has granted to us everything pertaining to life and godliness, through the true knowledge of Him who called us by His own glory and excellence"*. Note the difference? It says that His divine power has given us everything we need for life and godliness. The Bible teaches and exhorts us to allow the divine power of the Holy Spirit to do His work through us, but the Bible does not do the work. That's why it's so important to seek all the gifts that God bestows on us.

Now, I have one last argument to put forth. If the "supernatural gifts" have passed away since the time the canon of Scripture was completed, then there should not have been even one occurrence of those gifts operating in any person. I know this cannot be the case, since I have personally experienced some of those gifts operating in me from time to time. One might make the case that it could still happen occasionally, as it did in the Old Testament, when the Holy Spirit came upon an individual, but that would defeat the purpose of the gifts, which is to operate in, edify, and unify the Body of Christ.

You see, there is still practical need for words of knowledge, wisdom, gifts of healing and such in the body of Christ today. Just ask any missionary in primitive cultures, where medical technology is not readily available, about the need for miraculous healings. Where there is much demonic activity, discernment of spirits is immensely important. In counseling, a word of knowledge from the Lord may be necessary to solve a relationship problem when one person is not being open or truthful. I have personally had this experience on many occasions of counseling.

Maybe you've had times where you felt the Lord was giving you a special word or wanting to use you to accomplish a miracle or healing. We shouldn't be afraid to operate in any of the gifts of the Spirit just because we have seen abuse. I know that when God has done these kinds of works in my life, it has been an enormous blessing to see others in the body edified, and it can be for you as well.

Remember, God, through the Apostle Paul, instructs us to earnestly seek all of these gifts, then accept what He gives us. If we are relying on the Holy Spirit to bestow the gifts He wishes to, why should we have any apprehension? Jesus said that if we ask the Father for bread, would He give us a stone? The answer is, of course not. (Mt 7:9-12) Remember also that the purpose of gifts is to allow the body of Christ to operate at maximum efficiency. They are not just for your personal benefit.

Use of Gifts in the early church services

Before we examine each of the gifts, let's take a look at what an early church gathering may have been like. This will help us gain a better understanding of how the gifts might be used properly today. Most scholars agree that an early church service was a bit different than those held today. Gatherings were smaller, probably most were in homes (1 Cor 16:19) and it's likely there was not an established order of service. That may be why Paul had to give so many instructions, especially to the church at Corinth. Let's look at some passages that give us an insight into what took place in these meetings.

Acts 20:7, NIV— *"on the first day of the week we came together to break bread. Paul spoke to the people and, because he intended to leave the next day, kept on talking until midnight."*

1 Cor 14:26, NIV— *"What then shall we say, brothers? When you come together, everyone has a hymn, or a word of instruction, a revelation, a tongue or an interpretation. All of these must be done*

for the strengthening of the church. If anyone speaks in a tongue, two — or at the most three — should speak, one at a time, and someone must interpret. If there is no interpreter, the speaker should keep quiet in the church and speak to himself and God. Two or three prophets should speak, and the others should weigh carefully what is said. And if a revelation comes to someone who is sitting down, the first speaker should stop. For you can all prophesy in turn so that everyone may be instructed and encouraged. The spirits of prophets are subject to the control of prophets. For God is not a God of disorder but of peace. As in all the congregations of the saints, women should remain silent in the churches. They are not allowed to speak, but must be in submission, as the Law says. If they want to inquire about something, they should ask their own husbands at home; for it is disgraceful for a woman to speak in the church. Did the word of God originate with you? Or are you the only people it has reached? If anybody thinks he is a prophet or spiritually gifted, let him acknowledge that what I am writing to you is the Lord's command. If he ignores this, he himself will be ignored. Wherefore, brethren, covet to prophesy, and forbid not to speak in languages. Let all things be done decently, and in order."

Acts 13:1-3, NIV— *"Now there were at Antioch, in the church that was there, prophets and teachers: Barnabas, and Simeon who was called Niger, and Lucius of Cyrene, and Manaen who had been brought up with Herod the tetrarch, and Saul. While they were ministering to the Lord and fasting, the Holy Spirit said, "Set apart for Me Barnabas and Saul for the work to which I have called them." Then, when they had fasted and prayed and laid their hands on them, they sent them away."*

It seems these early services were very participatory. Those who were giving the prophecies may have been foretelling, but they may also have been explaining the prophecies that had been given by Jesus and the Apostles. We do know that as the church developed, teaching became of utmost importance.

1 Tim. 4: 11, NIV— *"Command and teach these things. Don't let anyone look down on you because you are young, but set an example for the believers in speech, in life, in love, in faith and in purity.*

Until I come, devote yourself to the public reading of Scripture, to preaching and to teaching. Do not neglect your gift, which was given you through a prophetic message when the body of elders laid their hands on you. Be diligent in these matters; give yourself wholly to them, so that everyone may see your progress. Watch your life and doctrine closely. Persevere in them, because if you do, you will save both yourself and your hearers."

You may ask, "Why do our services have less participation than what we see here?" You can see that though this might work well in smaller group situations, it could become chaotic in a big congregation. Paul did go about appointing elders in the churches to lead them, but we really don't have a lot of other information on what took place in the actual meetings. We do know from Acts 2 and Hebrews 10:25 how important gathering together as believers was and is.

PART 2

EXAMINING EACH GIFT

Now that we have seen that all of the listed gifts are operating today, let's examine each one. I want to start with the two gifts that the apostle Paul spent the most time explaining: prophecy and tongues. We aren't sure why Paul spent so much more time on these two gifts than the others, but it's possible that it was their abuse and need for correction that prompted him. You will see that as we go through the scriptures concerning them. It is also interesting that he seemed to speak about them together, comparing and contrasting their purpose in the body and instructing the church in their proper use.

Prophecy: (***propheteia***) Most Greek scholars agree this has two applications. It can mean to foretell events, or to speak under divine inspiration (forth telling, which is tantamount to preaching and explaining the prophetic scriptures) and accompanies the prophetic office. Look at 1 Corinthians 12:28— *"And God has appointed in the church, first apostles, second prophets, third teachers, then miracles, then gifts of healings, helps, administrations, various kinds of tongues."*

Scripture teaches that prophecy is not subject to a prophet's own interpretation— *"So we have the prophetic word made more sure, to which you do well to pay attention as to a lamp shining in a dark place, until the day dawns and the morning star arises in your hearts. But know this first of all, that no prophecy of Scripture is a matter of one's own interpretation, for no prophecy was ever made by an act of human will, but men moved by the Holy Spirit spoke from God"* (2 Peter 1:19-21, NIV).

That means that there is a correct interpretation for all prophecy. If a person is truly exercising the gift of prophecy in either sense of the word, the interpretation will be correct because it is from God himself by the power of the Holy Spirit.

Under the Old Covenant, God spoke to the nation of Israel through the prophets. This is recorded in many of the Old Testament passages. For about four hundred years, before the birth of Jesus Christ, God was silent. Then God began to speak again through prophets, beginning with Zacharias, the father of John the Baptist. This continued with John himself and of course Jesus. After Pentecost, we see many examples of the gift of prophecy operating in Peter, Paul, and others.

No distinction is made on who may receive this gift. Though we see it operating often in the apostles, there is mention of others. Agabus in Acts 11:28-30— *"One of them named Agabus stood up and began to indicate by the Spirit that there would certainly be a great famine all over the world. And this took place in the reign of Claudius. And in the proportion that any of the disciples had means, each of them determined to send a contribution for the relief of the brethren living in Judea. And this they did, sending it in charge of Barnabas and Saul to the elders."* Agabus also prophesies in Acts 21:10 and a woman, Anna, is spoken of in Luke 2:36. Just as in the Old Testament, there are males and females using the gift of prophecy.

So, what did Paul teach about how this gift should operate in the church? Look at 1 Corinthians 14:29-33— *"Two or three prophets should speak, and the others should weigh carefully what is said. And if a revelation comes to someone who is sitting down, the first speaker should stop. For you can all prophesy in turn so that everyone may be instructed and encouraged. The spirits of prophets are subject to the control of prophets. For God is not a God of disorder but of peace"* (NIV). We clearly see that he is speaking in terms of the church service.

As mentioned in chapter one, it would seem that in the early church, many people participated in church gatherings and that, at times, prophecies were spoken. We don't know for sure, but I would surmise that this was a combination of foretelling and preaching.

Note that Paul was adamant about order in the church service and that prophecies were to be "carefully weighed."

Remember that false prophecies are an abomination to God. He never wants to be misrepresented. Under the Old Covenant, any false prophecy was serious business. If it led to rebellion against the Lord, it was worthy of capital punishment. (Dt 13:1-5, 18:20-22) Notice also that in verse 31, Paul tells us what purpose prophecy is to serve. He says it is for *instruction* and *encouragement*. Can you see why it's so important that prophecy is not subject to the prophet's own interpretation? There has to be a correct interpretation in order to instruct properly and encourage correctly.

What else did Paul have to say about this gift?

1. If anyone thinks they have the gift, they should acknowledge that Paul's teaching about it is from the Lord (1 Cor 14:37).
2. Be eager to prophesy (v. 39).
3. Eagerly desire the gift (v. 1).
4. Rather that a person prophesy than speak in tongues. (v. 5).
5. One who prophesies is greater than one who speaks in tongues unless the speaker has an interpreter (v. 5).
6. The church is edified by prophecy (v. 5).
7. It is to be used in proportion to one's faith (Rom 12:6).

Use in the church today

Considering all the teaching by Paul, it would seem that the most useful purpose of prophecy today is in the teaching of God's word. That would include the "forth telling" aspect of prophecy, being able to explain clearly the prophecies that have been fulfilled and those that are yet to be fulfilled. Certainly a teaching pastor would need this gift. It isn't enough just to learn by studying. To be "taught" and led by the Holy Spirit is essential in order to instruct others in any area.

We should not, however, exclude the possibility that God may speak about an event through someone exercising this gift. Paul says that we are to "weigh carefully" what is said. What do we weigh it against? We weigh it against the Scriptures. This is extremely important, because we are warned that false prophets will come among the church and introduce destructive heresies (2 Pt 2:1). If the prophecy does not line up with God's revealed Word, it must be rejected. Remember, prophecy is God speaking to man and He will not contradict Himself.

Another question often asked is, "does the office of prophet still exist today?" That's a good question. I guess we would have to define what the office of prophet really is. Under the Old Covenant it was pretty easy to recognize who the prophets were. They spoke for God and whatever they said came true. There are certainly a number of prophets mentioned in the book of Acts. It seems that Paul places a great importance on the office, as it is second only to apostleship on his list in 1 Corinthians (12:28) and Ephesians (2:20, 3:5, 4:11). Personally, I wouldn't take a dogmatic position on this, but after the church had been established, there may not have been need for the office of a prophet. Look at Heb 1:1-3— " *In the past God spoke to our forefathers through the prophets at many times and in various ways, but in these last days he has spoken to us by his Son, whom he appointed heir of all things, and through whom he made the universe. The Son is the radiance of God's glory and the exact representation of his being, sustaining all things by his powerful word.*"

Some would hold the position that a Pastor/Teacher holds the office of prophet as well.

I would just say this. If someone feels the need to call himself a prophet, I would be very skeptical of that claim. I don't see prophets in the Bible introduce themselves by saying, "Hi, I am the prophet Gaius. Nice to meet you, now let me tell you the future of the world." One thing we can be sure of is that there will be two prophets who appear in the world again and they will not only prophesy, but that they will have great powers similar to the Old Testament prophets. You can read about them in Revelation, chapter 11.

It's easy to see how the gift of prophecy is used to edify the body of Christ. A Pastor/Teacher with this gift (in its' forth telling sense) can explain the fulfillment of prophesies as well as what the future holds according to the Bible. In a foretelling sense, it could be used to help direct people to follow God's leading. It could be used to warn people of situations or encourage them by confirming something they believed God was calling them to do. Again, it is critical to be sure a prophecy is from the Lord by testing it against Scripture.

Tongues: (*glossa*) NT:1100 of uncertain affinity; the tongue; by implication, a language (specially, one naturally unacquired) [6]

The highly regarded German translator, Kittle, says this about the Greek word for "tongues," NT: 1100 "An expression which in speech or manner is strange and obscure and needs explanation" [7] He also states that the word glossolalia referred to a "spiritually effected speaking, not to men but to God (emphasis mine). This is critical to our understanding of this gift.

Let's look at the scriptures concerning tongues so that we might come to a proper understanding of its purpose and correct use in the church today. The first example is one most teachers either purposely ignore or just don't think about and it is important because it is spoken by the Lord Jesus just before He ascended into heaven. Mark 16:15-- He said to them, *"Go into all the world and preach the good news to all creation. Whoever believes and is baptized will be saved, but whoever does not believe will be condemned. And these signs will accompany those who believe: In my name they will drive out demons; they will speak in new tongues; they will pick up snakes with their hands; and when they drink deadly poison, it will not hurt them at all; they will place their hands on sick people, and they will get well"* (NIV).

Note the word, new (NT: 2537 kainos (kahee-nos'); of uncertain affinity; new (especially in freshness;) [8]

It is possible, that since Jesus was speaking directly to the eleven remaining disciples, that He meant this only for them, but since it happened to others in the rest of Acts, we should not assume this. By the way, He was not teaching people to purposely pick up snakes; He was simply saying that in the course of ministry, sometimes a person will be protected from injury. This happened to the apostle Paul, who interestingly enough was not present at the time Jesus said this.

Instances of tongues:

Acts 2:1-11--*"When the day of Pentecost had come, they were all together in one place. And suddenly there came from heaven a noise like a violent rushing wind, and it filled the whole house where they were sitting. And there appeared to them tongues as of fire distributing themselves, and they rested on each one of them. And they were all filled with the Holy Spirit and began to speak with other tongues, as the Spirit was giving them utterance.*

Now there were Jews living in Jerusalem, devout men from every nation under heaven. And when this sound occurred, the crowd came together and were bewildered because each one of them was hearing them speak in his own language. They were amazed and astonished, saying, 'Why, are not all these who are speaking Galileans? And how is it that we each hear them in our own language to which we were born? Parthians and Medes and Elamites, and residents of Mesopotamia, Judea and Cappadocia, Pontus and Asia, Phrygia and Pamphylia, Egypt and the districts of Libya around Cyrene, and visitors from Rome, both Jews and proselytes, Cretans and Arabs — we hear them in our own tongues speaking of the mighty deeds of God.'"

Note that in this instance, the languages spoken were known languages, but not known to those who were speaking them.

Acts 10:44-48--*"While Peter was still speaking these words, the Holy Spirit fell upon all those who were listening to the message. All the circumcised believers who came with Peter were amazed, because the gift of the Holy Spirit had been poured out on the Gentiles also. For they were hearing them speaking with tongues and exalting God. Then Peter answered, 'Surely no one can refuse the water for these to be baptized who have received the Holy Spirit just as we did, can he?' And he ordered them to be baptized in the name of Jesus Christ. Then they asked him to stay on for a few days."*

This event gave proof that Gentiles could be saved and receive the Holy Spirit. The languages may or may not have been known, but it was evident that they were praising God. How was this known? It seems as though there must have been someone there who had the gift of interpretation of tongues. It is important to see here that this was not a church service but a gathering of believers having a theological discussion concerning God's desire to save Gentiles as well as Jews. This is important. I will explain why in just a bit.

Acts 19:1-7--*It happened that while Apollos was at Corinth, Paul passed through the upper country and came to Ephesus, and found some disciples. He said to them, "Did you receive the Holy Spirit when you believed?" And they said to him, "No, we have not even heard whether there is a Holy Spirit." And he said, "Into what then were you baptized?" And they said, "Into John's baptism." Paul said, "John baptized with the baptism of repentance, telling the people to believe in Him who was coming after him, that is, in Jesus." When they heard this, they were baptized in the name of the Lord Jesus. And when Paul had laid his hands upon them, the Holy Spirit came on them, and they began speaking with tongues and prophesying.*

In this instance, prophecy accompanied speaking in tongues.

Paul's instructions about tongues

"All do not speak with tongues, do they?" (1Cor 12:30). Pretty clear don't you think?

"If I speak with the tongues of men and of angels, but do not have love, I have become a noisy gong or a clanging cymbal" (1 Cor 13:1). Any doubt about what he is trying to point out here?

*"For anyone who speaks in a tongue **does not speak to men but to God**. Indeed, no one understands him; **he utters mysteries with his spirit**."* (1Cor 14:2, NIV, Emphasis mine).

"He who speaks in a tongue edifies himself" (1 Cor 14:4, NIV).

"...He who prophesies is greater than one who speaks in tongues, unless he interprets, so that the church may be edified" (1 Cor 14:5, NIV).

"For this reason anyone who speaks in a tongue should pray that he may interpret what he says. For if I pray in a tongue, my spirit prays, but my mind is unfruitful. So what shall I do? I will pray with my spirit, but I will also pray with my mind; I will sing with my spirit, but I will also sing with my mind. If you are praising God with your spirit, how can one who finds himself among those who do not understand say "Amen" to your thanksgiving, since he does not know what you are saying? You may be giving thanks well enough, but the other man is not edified. I thank God that I speak in tongues more than all of you. But in the church I would rather speak five intelligible words to instruct others than ten thousand words in a tongue." (1Cor 14:13-19, NIV).

Tongues then, are a sign, not for believers but for unbelievers; prophecy, however, is for believers, not for unbelievers. *So if the whole church comes together and everyone speaks in tongues, and some who do not understand or some unbelievers come in, will they not say that you are out of your mind?* ***But if an unbeliever or someone who does not understand comes in while everybody is prophesying, he will be convinced by all that he is a sinner and will be judged by all,*** *and the secrets of his heart will be laid bare. So he will fall down and worship God, exclaiming, "God is really among you!"*

"What then shall we say, brothers? When you come together, everyone has a hymn, or a word of instruction, a revelation, a tongue or an interpretation. All of these must be done for the strengthening of the church. ***If anyone speaks in a tongue, two — or at the most three — should speak, one at a time, and someone must interpret. If there is no interpreter, the speaker should keep quiet in the church and speak to himself and God."*** (1 Cor 14:22-28, NIV, emphasis mine)

Now, if this seems somewhat confusing to you, don't feel bad. Many good biblical scholars have been confused as well. It seems as if Paul is contradicting himself. In verse 22 he says tongues is a sign for unbelievers, not believers, but he then says in the very next verse that if unbelievers come into the church and hear everyone speaking in tongues they might think that those people are crazy.

Let me explain. We see in Scripture that there are two applications of the gift of tongues, just as there are two aspects of the gift of prophecy. In verse 18 and 19 Paul says, "I thank God that I speak in tongues more than all of you. But in the church I would rather speak five intelligible words to instruct others than ten thousand words in a tongue."

You see here, Paul is explaining the use of the gift of tongues in application to the body. He obviously spoke in tongues at times other than in a church service. Remember, tongues are man speaking to God. He used tongues mostly in private, where its' main purpose is fulfilled. There is no need for interpretation since a person is speaking to God. I am pretty sure He knows what is being said. Many people refer to this as the private prayer language that God has gifted them with.

Look at Romans 8:26-27: *"In the same way, the Spirit helps us in our weakness. We do not know what we ought to pray for, but the Spirit himself intercedes for us with groans that words cannot express. And he who searches our hearts knows the mind of the Spirit, because the Spirit intercedes for the saints in accordance with God's will"* (NIV). Some teach that this has nothing to do with tongues because it says groans, which is not a language. That is true, but I am not too sure that Paul is saying that is necessarily different. Look how he puts it in 1 Corinthians 14:2-3: *"For one who speaks in a tongue does not speak to men but to God; for no one understands, but in his spirit he speaks mysteries."* In both cases, you will note that it is the Spirit who is directing the prayer, interceding to help a person communicate with God the Father.

First Corinthians 14:4 said that the one who speaks in tongues edifies himself. It is not meant for teaching in the church. Even if it is interpreted, it is man speaking to God. Now, there could be some encouragement for others when they understand what was prayed, just as when you pray in the common language and something is spoken to God that encourages or even instructs you. That is what

Paul is alluding to here. Again, the application of this gift is better served privately than in a church service but that does not mean it has no place in a gathering of believers. It just needs to be interpreted. If the speaker does not have the gift of interpretation and does not know if there is one present that can interpret, it is better to remain silent.

How does that square with what we learned about the purpose of spiritual gifts being to edify the body, not just serve ourselves? Well, think about it. When you are encouraged by the Lord in your prayer life, doesn't that help you to encourage and bless others? When you spend intimate time with the Lord, don't you grow stronger and then desire to help others do the same? This gift, when used properly, will benefit the whole body.

Ok, now for the second application. When is this gift used as a sign for unbelievers? Well, we know for sure that it happened in Acts 2. When Jews from all over the region saw believers speaking in tongues that were not theirs (but were known languages), it got their attention. Then Peter explained what was going on and three thousand people got saved! Pretty useful sign, don't you think?

Tongues were also used as a sign to unbelieving Jews that Paul's message of salvation was for all who believe, including Gentiles. Read Acts 10:44-47, 19:1-7. The key verse to understanding this is not often taught. Look at Verse 21 in 1 Corinthians 14. *"In the Law it is written: "Through men of strange tongues and through the lips of foreigners I will speak to this people, but even then they will not listen to me," says the Lord"* (NIV). This is a reference (Is 28:11-12) to times in the Old Testament where God used foreign people with foreign languages to bring a message of forthcoming judgment to Israel but they would not listen. (Note again that these were known languages but not understood by the Jews. In Acts, many did listen and chose to follow the Lord. But once again, the majority of the Jewish people rejected the message and will face judgment.

There is one more controversy that I can hopefully to lay to rest for good in your mind about tongues. The question always seems to arise when dealing with the subject of tongues, "Is speaking in tongues the evidence that you have been saved by Christ?" Though some people teach this, it is completely false. After reading all the scriptures that have already been set forth here, I am hopeful that you have already reached that conclusion. Just look again at what Paul said to Corinthian believers: "All do not speak with tongues, do they?" (1Cor 12:30). How much more clearly could Paul say it? Not all believers will speak in tongues; therefore, it has nothing to do with whether or not a person is saved.

Use in the church today

To sum up what we have discovered in the Scriptures, the primary purpose for the gift of tongues to believers today is to help them in speaking to God, especially in their private prayer time. When used properly, it can enhance a believer's personal time with the Lord and certainly encourage his or her walk with Him. In turn, that believer can encourage others. If used in a service, it must be orderly and interpretation must follow. That can also be an encouragement to other believers.

Outside of the church setting, it could be used as a sign to unbelievers. This would seem to be a spontaneous outpouring of the Holy Spirit. I don't really see this happening today and if it did and followed the pattern in the Bible, it would seem to happen as a sign to Jewish non-believers.

Interpretation of Tongues (The Greek root word for interpretation is *hermeneuo,* which simply means to translate.)

We really don't have much else to go on here. All we know is that in the church service, if people are speaking in tongues, known or unknown languages, someone should be present with that gift to translate. It could be that a person speaks in a language they don't know, but there is someone present who does know that language and interprets. It could also be an unknown language that God reveals to the person who has the gift of interpretation. The problem with this is that we can't always be sure it is accurate. Since the purpose of tongues is to help man speak to God, we do know that the prayers must glorify Him.

Gifts (Charisma; endowment, religious qualification or miraculous faculty) of **Healing** (NT: 2386 iama; from NT: 2390; a cure (the effect): NT: 2390 iaomai (ee-ah'-om-ahee); middle voice of apparently a primary verb; to cure (literally or figuratively) [9]

By definition, we see that the exercise of this gift brings about a cure for sickness, disease, disability, or injury. This word is one that is used in some of the healings that were performed by Jesus, but not all. It is only used twice in conjunction with the healings we see in the book of Acts. In many other cases, a different Greek word is used to describe the healing. That word is (therapeuo), which also means to cure or serve. Since both words have the same primary meaning, I don't believe it denotes any significant difference. They seem to be used interchangeably.

Iaomai is used, however, in a very important verse when Peter was describing the ministry of Jesus--Acts 10:38: *"You know of Jesus of Nazareth, how God anointed Him with the Holy Spirit and with power, and how He went about doing good and healing all who were oppressed by the devil, for God was with Him."*

I think that this is important because it corroborates the fact that the gifts of healing accomplish the same purposes that Jesus had. Some were healed from sickness, diseases, etc., but others were healed from demonic possession. Could it be that this is why Paul used the plural word "gifts" of healing? In any case, all of these healings were meant to bring glory to God. Let's look at some examples of healing in the book of Acts.

Acts 3:1-10--*Now Peter and John were going up to the temple at the ninth hour, the hour of prayer. And a man who had been lame from his mother's womb was being carried along, whom they used to set down every day at the gate of the temple which is called Beautiful, in order to beg alms of those who were entering the temple. When he saw Peter and John about to go into the temple, he began asking to receive alms. But Peter, along with John, fixed his gaze on him and said, "Look at us!" And he began to give them his attention, expecting to receive something from them. But Peter said, "I do not possess silver and gold, but what I do have I give to you: In the name of Jesus Christ the Nazarene — walk!" And seizing him by the right hand, he raised him up; and immediately his feet and his ankles were strengthened. With a leap he stood upright and began to walk; and he entered the temple with them, walking and leaping and praising God. And all the people saw him walking and praising God; and they were taking note of him as being the one who used to sit at the Beautiful Gate of the temple to beg alms, and they were filled with wonder and amazement at what had happened to him.*

Acts 5:15-16-- *to such an extent that they even carried the sick out into the streets and laid them on cots and pallets, so that when Peter came by at least his shadow might fall on any one of them. Also the people from the cities in the vicinity of Jerusalem were coming together, bringing people who were sick or afflicted with unclean spirits, and they were all being healed.*

Acts 8:5-7-*Philip went down to the city of Samaria and began proclaiming Christ to them. The crowds with one accord were giving attention to what was said by Philip, as they heard and saw the signs which he was performing. For in the case of many who had unclean spirits, they were coming out of them shouting with a loud voice; and many who had been paralyzed and lame were healed.*

Acts 28:8-9-*And it happened that the father of Publius was lying in bed afflicted with recurrent fever and dysentery; and Paul went in to see him and after he had prayed, he laid his hands on him and healed him. After this had happened, the rest of the people on the island who had diseases were coming to him and getting cured.*

Paul does not give us much more information about the gifts of healing, but the healings done by Jesus and those mentioned in Acts offer a few principles to consider.

1. Methods don't matter. If you look into all the healings that Jesus did and those in Acts, you will see that there is no consistent way that they took place. The only thing that matters is following the Lord's instruction. If He chooses to use a person in this way, that person should be obedient to the instructions God is giving him/her.
2. Faith is important. It may be the faith of the person being healed that is instrumental (Mt 9:22), the faith of others around a person (Mt 9:2), or the faith of the person doing the healing (Acts 3:1-10).
3. When we see healing take place in the New Testament, it is complete and visible (too many examples to list).
4. Not all healing takes place by people with this gift (Jas 5:14-16).
5. Not all healing has to be in the "miraculous" sense. Often God uses doctors and medicine (1 Tm 5:23).

Use in the church today

Since we believe that all of the gifts are given for the edification of the church, then this gift should be exercised for the same reason. A person who has the gift should use it when prompted by the Holy Spirit and be obedient to what he or she believes God is saying.

Since we see that people are healed in ways other than people exercising these gifts, why would it be necessary for anyone to have them? Back in chapter one, I gave some reasons. There are many times when there are no other options available. Maybe there is no doctor available or proper medicine on hand. Often there is no medical cure for a disease. Sometimes God just wants to make the point that He has the power to heal when He chooses. He gets the glory, people's faith may grow, and the church is edified.

I think the biggest mistake we make in reference to the gifts of healing is to overanalyze and become too methodical in how it is applied. If God is prompting you to pray, lay hands on someone, or obey a certain instruction in order for someone to be healed, you follow His leading. Just be sure your motivation is pure, that you are not seeking glory for yourself but trying to be obedient to Him.

Miraculous Powers or Working (*energeo*; to be active, efficient) of **Miracles** (doo'-nam-is; force, miraculous power). You can see that the words together could be translated as energy and miraculous power. Paul doesn't say much more in terms of describing this gift. I believe he assumes the reader has a good understanding of what it is. In the time this was written, not much explanation was needed. People had either seen or heard of the miracles of Jesus and the apostles. Obviously the healings that were performed were considered miraculous, but since that is a gift in itself, what other types of miracles do we see in the New Testament?

One of the most famous miracles (and most likely the first) was in John 2:1-11. This was the wedding in Cana, where Jesus turned water into wine. Jesus seemed to perform this miracle reluctantly. In John 2:4, He says, "'Dear woman, why do you involve me?' Jesus replied. 'My time has not yet come.'" This is important in understanding the main purpose of miracles. The miracles Jesus performed were to authenticate His ministry and His claim to be the Son of God and God in the flesh. It was also to reveal His glory. Jesus indicated that this was not yet the time to reveal that to the general public. He would first reveal Himself to His disciples and we are told in verse 11 and that after this miracle, they put their faith in Him. Now we know, looking back on it, that their faith at this point was not very strong, but it was a beginning.

Another miracle Jesus used to authenticate His ministry to His disciples is recorded in Luke 5:1-11. Jesus used this occasion to once again reveal His power and authority but at the end, He also uses it to encourage Peter to the ministry that Peter is to have later. This is important because it shows that when a person uses this gift, it can edify the body by encouraging others to use their gifts to accomplish the work God has for them.

Jesus used another miracle, calming the storm (Mt 8:23-27), to teach the disciples a lesson in faith. He does it again in Matthew 14:22-33, only this time He walks on the water as well. He asks Peter to take a step of faith, and Peter does, but unfortunately, it does not last long. Jesus then asks Peter, "Why did you doubt?" It is a lesson for us as well. If the Holy Spirit chooses us to participate in a miracle, will it fall short because of our lack of belief? As I mentioned earlier concerning use of the gift of healing, the working of miracles takes faith. Not faith in faith itself as some teach, or faith in any ability we possess, but faith in Jesus. He has the power to perform anything He desires through us, but having faith in Him and His ability to accomplish it is essential.

Consider the words of John 14:12-- *"I tell you the truth, anyone who has faith in me will do what I have been doing. He will do even greater things than these, because I am going to the Father. And I will do whatever you ask in my name, so that the Son may bring glory to the Father. 14 You may ask me for anything in my name, and I will do it."*

As faith is essential to accomplishing miracles by the power of the Spirit, so lack of faith is a hindrance. Remember this instance in Matthew 13:57-58? *"...A prophet is not without honor except in his hometown and in his own household." And He did not do many miracles there because of their unbelief."* Note that the passage does not say that He could not do the miracles because of unbelief. It says that He did not do them. This is an important distinction because many teachers in the "Word of Faith" movement teach that we can prevent God from doing what He wants to do, because we do not have enough faith. That is completely wrong. Unbelief is the opposite of faith. It did not simply mean they did not believe He could do miracles. In fact, they probably did believe He could do miracles. They had likely heard of His miraculous power. It was their unbelief in Him as Messiah that caused Him to choose not to do miracles. That is why He states that a prophet has honor everywhere but His own house and His own country. Those in His own hometown could not accept that He was more than the carpenter's son they watched grow up. They were steeped in unbelief. The majority of His own family did not even believe in Him until after the Resurrection!

Jesus performed many other miracles, not the least of which was raising Lazarus from the dead (Jn 11). In all cases, He was affirming who He was and His power over all creation, authenticating His teaching, and encouraging people to trust Him. When the Apostles did miracles, by the power of the Spirit, in the name of Jesus, they did essentially the same thing.

1. Acts 9:40 – Peter raises Dorcas or Tabitha from the dead. When this became known, people believed in the Lord.
2. Acts 5:12 says that the apostles performed many miraculous signs and wonders and that more and more people believed in the Lord and were added to their number.
3. Acts 5:3-11 is often used as a warning against deception in the church. Ananias and Sapphira paid with their life for their deception.
4. Acts 13:11-12 -- Two purposes were accomplished as Paul, by the power of the Spirit, strikes the deceitful and wicked Elymas with blindness. Satan's attempt at opposing God's plan is thwarted and, according to verse 12, the proconsul of that area became a believer.

Use in the church today

I see no reason to believe there would be any difference in how the working of miracles should operate today as opposed to in the early church or even by Jesus Himself. We need to keep in mind some important principles to make sure the gift is used properly. It should always be:

1. Done through the power of God (Jn 3:2; Acts 14:3, 15:12, 19:11)
2. Of the Spirit (Mt 12:28; Rom 15:19; 1 Cor 12:9-10,28,30)
3. In the name of Jesus Christ (Mk 16:17; Acts 3:16, 4:30)

Also, it is important that they are accomplishing the same purposes that we saw in the Gospels and the book of Acts:

1. Affirming the deity of Jesus
2. Revealing His power and His glory, not ours
3. Glorifying Him alone
4. Attesting to the truth of His Word
5. Encouraging non-believers to faith in Christ
6. Encouraging believers to a deeper faith and trust in Christ
7. Warning and possibly even judgment upon false and deceptive people who would try to thwart the purposes of God (Word of caution: if we look in Acts, we see this done only by the apostles and that even seems rare. Remember that all the

other principles we see in the Bible must be followed as well, from the wisdom of Proverbs to the teaching on judgment, forgiveness, and grace.)

If these purposes are accomplished, it will certainly be edifying to the church. If that is so, and since we see through the previously mentioned verses that this gift is for today's church, the question arises, "why do these miracles and healings seem to occur so rarely?" That is a very good question. It is a question that no one can answer with complete certainty. Let me offer you some thoughts on it.

If you take the Bible as a whole, written over a period of several thousand years, there are not that many healings and miracles recorded there, either. I am certain that more took place than what was recorded, but it still seems they have always been somewhat rare. At certain times it seems God uses them in clusters to achieve very specific ends, e.g.: Plagues of Egypt to bring the Hebrew nation out of bondages and then the miracles, signs, and wonders that helped lead them to the Promised Land.

Many miracles accompanied warnings and judgments in the books of the prophets so the people would know it was God himself speaking to them. Miracles surrounded the birth and ministry of Jesus, authenticating His deity. Many miracles accompanied the building of the church. Perhaps this is a pattern for when God wants to do a special work.

It could be, at least here in the western world, that unbelief has hindered the work of the Spirit in this way. We are trained to believe that there is a "scientific and rational answer" for everything that takes place. We could hang out a sign that says, "Miracles Not Welcome Here." Remember, when Jesus did not do many miracles in Nazareth, it wasn't because He couldn't; it was because of unbelief. I believe that means it would not have accomplished the purposes that miracles should accomplish because people would not believe in them. I specifically said "in the western world" because there are many documented miracles taking place all over other parts of the world today. In other cultures, they don't seem to have as much of a problem believing in miracles.

These are just some ideas but you might have others. I think the key is to be open to God's ability to bestow this gift to anyone at any time He desires and not worry about how often it occurs. That is up to Him!

Serving (*diakonia*): There are several uses of this word. It can mean to run errands or wait tables, it might refer to the servant of a master, or it might be figurative to describe a servant of a spiritual power. Interestingly, the King James Version of the Bible uses the term "ministry" For this word. The meaning is clear. It refers to all kinds of service to the body of Christ. The best example of this is in Acts 6. Let's look at Acts 6:1-4: *"In those days when the number of disciples was increasing, the Grecian Jews among them complained against the Hebraic Jews because their widows were being overlooked in the daily distribution of food. So the Twelve gathered all the disciples together and said, "It would not be right for us to neglect the ministry of the word of God in order to wait on tables. Brothers, choose seven men from among you who are known to be full of the Spirit and wisdom. We will turn this responsibility over to them and will give our attention to prayer and the ministry of the word"* (NIV).

This demonstrated the need for people to do the work of ministry outside of teaching, leadership, and administration. This did not limit them to "menial tasks." This particular gift was very important to the health of the growing church. By people gifted in this area doing what they do best and with a joyous spirit, others are blessed and enabled to do what God has called them to do.

Use in the Church Today

This gift should operate in the very same manner today. I can tell you as a pastor and worship leader that without true servants, the work of the ministry would not get done! The exercising of this gift by people in the church is a tremendous blessing to all of the body. Imagine how all the occasions for fellowship would be affected if no one desired to cook the food, set up and tear down the chairs and tables, etc. What if no one wanted to run slides for the worship services? You can see how important this gift is.

Teaching (*didasko* – To teach): Kittle says that the term has the unambiguous sense of "to teach" or "to instruct." The word is used all throughout the gospels in relationship to Jesus' instructing those around Him, from His disciples, to the multitudes, to the Jewish leaders.

It goes without saying, that for a person to be an effective teacher of the Bible, there is more to it than just knowing the Word. There is a good illustration of this in the book of Acts: *"Meanwhile a Jew named Apollos, a native of Alexandria, came to Ephesus. He was a learned man, with a thorough knowledge of the Scriptures. He had been instructed in the way of the Lord, and he spoke with great fervor and taught about Jesus accurately, though he knew only the baptism of John. He began to speak boldly in the synagogue. When Priscilla and Aquila heard him, they invited him to their home and explained to him the way of God more adequately"* (Acts 18:24-26, NIV).

This event is followed in narrative by Paul exercising the gift of miracles and laying hands on a group of disciples who, like Apollos, only knew the baptism of John (repentance). As Paul does this, they receive the baptism or filling of the Holy Spirit. This is not coincidental. Even though the events happened in two different places, they are connected to teach us an important lesson. If you look at verse 28 in chapter 18 it tells us that Apollos could prove to the Jews from Scripture that Jesus was the Christ. It does not mention that this led to any conversions to Christ. Now it may not mean that none took place, but it seems that everywhere else in Acts we are told about salvations and adding to the Church.

I bring this up only to emphasize that anyone can and should read and know the Scriptures. The key for it being used to truly "instruct" lies in a person being filled with the Spirit and exercising a gift given to him by the Spirit--the gift of teaching.

We see this gift operating in the life of Paul throughout the book of Acts. There is a spiritual effect when a gifted teacher teaches. It results in conviction, encouragement, and desire for action on the part of the hearer. The gift should be nurtured and developed. Paul instructs the young pastor Timothy in the development and use of this gift in 1 and 2 Timothy as well as warning against false teachers. It is an absolute must for the pastor/elder to have this gift (1 Tm 3:2) and even though he prepares thoroughly, he must rely upon the Spirit to do the spiritual work.

One of the sobering facts about teaching is the high standard maintained for one who is operating in this gift. Let's look at James 3:1-2: *"Not many of you should presume to be teachers, my brothers, because you know that we who teach will be judged more strictly"* (NIV).

1 Tm 1:3-7 *"As I urged you upon my departure for Macedonia, remain on at Ephesus so that you may instruct certain men not to teach strange doctrines, nor to pay attention to myths and endless genealogies, which give rise to mere speculation rather than furthering the administration of God which is by faith. But the goal of our instruction is love from a pure heart and a good conscience and a sincere faith. For some men, straying from these things, have turned aside to fruitless discussion, wanting to be teachers of the Law, even though they do not understand either what they are saying or the matters about which they make confident assertions."*

Ti 2:1-2: *"You must teach what is in accord with sound doctrine"* (NIV).

Use in the Church Today

Since the office of pastor/elder/teacher is mentioned as one of the offices in Ephesians 4, it is essential that those who are gifted by the Holy Spirit to teach are obedient in exercising their gift in order for the church to function as "one body." It is a top priority, in order that the church be edified, for "gifted" teaching pastors to fill our pulpits today.

That is not the only place this gift should be operating, however. We need people with the gift of teaching in our Sunday School classes, small group studies, men's /women's ministries and worship teams, even if they are not necessarily gifted in all the areas that a Pastor/ Teacher is. Again, there are no restrictions on who receives this gift. Whoever has this gift should seek the proper place to use it.

Encouraging (*parakaleo*: to call near) this word is also translated as comfort, consolation, encouragement, urging, or exhortation. The idea is that a person with this gift uses it to bring all these attributes to others in the church. It is not just to bring a human form of comfort or encouragement, though. It is also to draw a person closer to the Lord. That is where the exhortation comes in. Let's look at some examples in the New Testament.

Acts 11:19: *"Now those who had been scattered by the persecution in connection with Stephen traveled as far as Phoenicia, Cyprus and Antioch, telling the message only to Jews. Some of them, however, men from Cyprus and Cyrene, went to Antioch and began to speak to Greeks also, telling them the good news about the Lord Jesus. The Lord's hand was with them, and a great number of people believed and turned to the Lord. News of this reached the ears of the church at Jerusalem, and they sent Barnabas to Antioch. When he arrived and saw the evidence of the grace of God, he was glad and encouraged them all to remain true to the Lord with all their hearts"* (NIV).

Acts 15:30: *"The men were sent off and went down to Antioch, where they gathered the church together and delivered the letter. The people read it and were glad for its encouraging message"* (NIV).

1 Thes 3:2: *"We sent Timothy, who is our brother and God's fellow worker in spreading the gospel of Christ, to strengthen and encourage you in your faith, so that no one would be unsettled by these trials"* (NIV).

2 Thes 2:16-17: *"May our Lord Jesus Christ himself and God our Father, who loved us and by his grace gave us eternal encouragement and good hope, encourage your hearts and strengthen you in every good deed and word"* (NIV).

What this shows us is that a person exercising this gift has the ability to comfort, encourage, and even confront when necessary in order to help others trust in God and His promises. These people posses a God-given ability to help draw people near to God. They use the Scriptures in a way that edifies (building up) and challenges when necessary to Godly living.

Use in the Church today

I see several applications of this gift today. I believe that teaching pastors should have this gift. Without it, they may be great teachers but might end up continually "beating the sheep," rather than encouraging them to "love and good deeds" (Heb 10:24).

The gift of encouragement is certainly not limited to pastors. Anyone in the church could receive and use it, but it behooves a person to whom God has graciously given this gift, to learn the Scriptures thoroughly in order to use it properly. It also means that the person using this gift needs to have a deep personal relationship with the Lord. Often when using this gift, what brings comfort, consolation, encouragement, and exhortation to people is being able to share how God has worked in his or her own life.

2 Cor 1:3 says, *"Praise be to the God and Father of our Lord Jesus Christ, the Father of compassion and the God of all comfort, 4 who comforts us in all our troubles, so that we can comfort those in any trouble with the comfort we ourselves have received from God"* (NIV).

Each time you see the word "comfort" in this verse, remember it is a form of *parakaleo*. Certainly the exercising of this gift properly is a blessing and edifies the body of Christ!

Giving (*metadidomi:* to share, to give over) the word here is only used a few times in the Bible. It is often translated as "share."

Lk 3:11: *"John answered, 'The man with two tunics should share with him who has none, and the one who has food should do the same'"* (NIV).

Eph 4:28: *"He who has been stealing must steal no longer, but must work, doing something useful with his own hands, that he may have something to share with those in need"* (NIV).

1 Thes 2:8: *"We loved you so much that we were delighted to share with you not only the gospel of God but our lives as well, because you had become so dear to us. Surely you remember, brothers, our toil and hardship; we worked night and day in order not to be a burden to anyone while we preached the gospel of God to you"* (NIV).

As you can see, this gift of giving means to share with those in need. It is not exclusively about giving your offering to the local church, however it certainly could be exercised in this way. I think the translation of thought in the NIV is accurate. Rom 12:8: *"if it is contributing to the needs of others, let him give generously."* That is the key to using this gift--giving generously.

Looking at Acts 2:43-47, we see the example of this concept.

"Everyone kept feeling a sense of awe; and many wonders and signs were taking place through the apostles. And all those who had believed were together and had all things in common; and they began selling their property and possessions and were sharing them with all, as anyone might have need. Day by day continuing with one mind in the temple, and breaking bread from house to house, they were taking their meals together with gladness and sincerity of heart, praising God and having favor with all the people. And the Lord was adding to their number day by day those who were being saved."

The early disciples were selling their possessions and goods in order to give to those in need. This was all voluntary. It was according to the work that the Holy Spirit was doing in their lives.

Use in the Church Today

What Paul emphasizes here in Romans is to be generous when exercising this gift. The King James Version says give with simplicity. Being a simple person, I like that. I believe the idea is that God blesses people with this gift, they give without overanalyzing it because they are led by the Spirit.

I have watched many who exercise this gift be blessed with more and more materially because they just continue to give it away. I have heard of businessmen who started out giving ten percent of their business income to the Lord and keeping the other 90 percent, but God so increased their profits that they give more and more until they are actually giving 90 percent and keeping 10 percent. This is definitely a biblical principal.

Look at 2 Cor 9:6-12 *"Now this I say, he who sows sparingly will also reap sparingly, and he who sows bountifully will also reap bountifully. Each one must do just as he has purposed in his heart, not grudgingly or under compulsion, for God loves a cheerful giver. And God is able to make all grace abound to you, so that always having all sufficiency in everything, you may have an abundance for every good deed; as it is written, 'HE SCATTERED ABROAD, HE GAVE TO THE POOR, HIS RIGHTEOUSNESS ENDURES FOREVER.' Now He who supplies seed to the sower and bread for food will supply and multiply your seed for sowing and increase the harvest of your righteousness; you will be enriched in everything for all liberality, which through us is producing thanksgiving to God."*

Those whom God has blessed with the gift of giving, in turn bless the Body of Christ by sharing in the provision God has blessed them with. Again, you will recognize the authenticity of the gift, when you see God receiving the glory, not the person exercising the gift.

Leadership (proistemi: to stand before, to preside. It is also translated as "manage," "have charge over," or "rule.") [10]This term is used in 1 Thes 5:12: *"Now we ask you, brothers, to respect those who work hard among you, who are over you in the Lord and who admonish you"* (NIV). This gives you the sense of what the word means as far as the church is concerned.

God has anointed leaders all throughout history. We see them in the Old Testament--Joseph, Moses, David, and many others. He did the same in the early church. We see Peter, Paul, James (brother of Jesus), John, and Paul's spiritual son, Timothy. When God calls someone to leadership, it is up to Him to give the ability to lead and that is done by the power of the Spirit. What Paul would say to those to whom God has bestowed this gift is, do it with "spoude," which means eagerness, speed, or earnestness.

Those who were exercising the gift of leadership in the early church are found in the offices that Paul talks about. It would include apostles, prophets, evangelists, and pastors/teachers, but was not limited to those. Priscilla, Aquila, and Phoebe seem to have been in positions of leadership (Ro 16:1). Remember that Priscilla and Aquila had to explain to Apollos about the Holy Spirit.

With the offices of leadership in the early church came requirements: Titus 1:6-9: *"An elder must be blameless, the husband of but one wife, a man whose children believe and are not open to the charge of being wild and disobedient. Since an overseer is entrusted with God's work, he must be blameless — not overbearing, not quick-tempered, not given to drunkenness, not violent, not pursuing dishonest gain. Rather he must be hospitable, one who loves what is good, who is self-controlled, upright, holy and disciplined. He must hold firmly to the trustworthy message as it has been taught, so that he can encourage others by sound doctrine and refute those who oppose it"* (NIV).

It is evident that there is great importance in the leaders of each local church meeting these requirements. When people who are entrusted with leadership do not have the integrity necessary to be trusted with that responsibility, much damage can occur. Satan loves to use leaders of churches to destroy God's work. Acts 20:29-31 says, *"I know that after my departure savage wolves will come in among you, not sparing the flock; and from among your own selves men will arise, speaking perverse things, to draw away the disciples after them."*

One of the other dangers in the church is that there are people who seem to have great leadership abilities, but may not be mature in the Lord or led by His Spirit. If they are put into a position of leadership, it becomes a disaster, often leading to much damage in a local church or even to the body as a whole. Remember, natural abilities are not always an indication of the bestowing of a spiritual gift.

One mistake often made in today's church is not following the instructions Paul has given concerning leadership in the body of Christ. The Bible contains clear directions for leadership in the church and as much as possible, they should be followed. God set the first rules of leadership down in the book of Genesis 3:16: *"...yet your desire will be for your husband, and he will rule over you."* Then Paul reiterated that, in order to qualify for leadership positions in the church, men would have to show that they are strong leaders in their home.

Jesus gave the most important rule for leadership to His disciples. Mark 10:42 says, *"Jesus called them together and said, 'You know that those who are regarded as rulers of the Gentiles lord it over them, and their high officials exercise authority over them. Not so with you. Instead, whoever wants to become great among you must be your servant, and whoever wants to be first must be slave of all. For even the Son of Man did not come to be served, but to serve, and to give his life as a ransom for many.'"* The true leaders in God's economy must have the heart of a servant!

Use in the Church Today

Without beginning a debate about denominations, which have a hierarchy of leadership beyond the local church, the most obvious use for the gift of leadership in the church today is equipping people to guide local church bodies. Paul appointed elders over the local churches to lead them. When those elders meet the qualifications set down by Paul and are led by the Spirit in using their gift of leadership, it is a true blessing to the local church, which is in turn a blessing to the whole body of Christ.

That being said, leadership in the church is not limited to the aforementioned offices. Leadership is needed in various ministries in the church. Worship, children's ministry, men's and women's ministry, you name it. If a person desires to lead a ministry, they need to have the gift of leadership, which can only be given by the Holy Spirit. They must maintain the attitude that Jesus had, demonstrating the heart of a servant.

Mercy (*eleeo*: compassion by word or deed, especially by divine grace, pity, sympathy, sometimes translated as "compassion" Mt 9:13) [11] The key to understanding this as a gift is realizing it is a term of action, showing mercy. The compassion one feels for others in their circumstances leads the person to act.

There are many examples of this in the ministry of Jesus:

Mt 9:27-29 *"As Jesus went on from there, two blind men followed Him, crying out, 'Have mercy on us, Son of David!' When He entered the house, the blind men came up to Him, and Jesus said to them, 'Do you believe that I am able to do this?' They said to Him, 'Yes, Lord.' Then He touched their eyes, saying, 'It shall be done to you according to your faith.'"*

Mt 15:22-28 *"And a Canaanite woman from that region came out and began to cry out, saying, 'Have mercy on me, Lord, Son of David; my daughter is cruelly demon-possessed.' But He did not answer her a word. And His disciples came and implored Him, saying, 'Send her away, because she keeps shouting at us.' But He answered and said, 'I was sent only to the lost sheep of the house of Israel.' But she came and began to bow down before Him, saying, 'Lord, help me!' And He answered and said, 'It is not good to take the children's bread and throw it to the dogs.' But she said, 'Yes, Lord; but even the dogs feed on the crumbs which fall from their masters' table.' Then Jesus said to her, 'O woman, your faith is great; it shall be done for you as you wish.' And her daughter was healed at once."*

Mt 17:15-18 *"'Lord, have mercy on my son, for he is a lunatic and is very ill; for he often falls into the fire and often into the water. 'I brought him to Your disciples, and they could not cure him.' And Jesus answered and said, 'You unbelieving and perverted generation, how long shall I be with you? How long shall I put up with you? Bring him here to Me.' And Jesus rebuked him, and the demon came out of him, and the boy was cured at once."*

Mercy is often associated with other gifts such as miracles, healing, and giving in its operation, as you can see in these verses. It was mercy that led Peter to heal the blind man in Acts 3.

Probably one of the best examples is the story of the Good Samaritan found in Luke 10:30-37. In this case, the Samaritan's mercy led to his care and generosity. In the Sermon on the Mount, Jesus said that those who are merciful would be shown mercy. It is very evident that God wants all of us to show mercy.

Use in the Church Today

How do we see mercy operating as a gift that edifies the body today? Since we are all supposed to be merciful, shouldn't everyone have that gift? That is a good question. Paul told us to pray for all the gifts, so certainly we should ask God for it. That does not mean that everyone will have mercy as a spiritual gift. How do we know if someone has this particular gift? Look at what Paul says in the text (Ro 12:8). When you show mercy, do it cheerfully. The Greek word means "with hilarity." When you see people operating in this gift, you will see it done cheerfully, with great joy. That should be true whenever we are operating in any gift God has given us.

The second way you recognize the spiritual gift of mercy operating in a person, is by their first response to someone's difficult circumstance. They respond by finding an action to take to try and help that person. Many of us feel compassion for people in trying times, but we do not always try to help. In fact, we might not even feel the compassion immediately that a person with the gift of mercy does. We might wonder if it is the right thing to do to help a particular person in their circumstance. That is ok because, as mentioned earlier, the body is supposed to work together. The person with the gift of mercy always wants to help, which is good, but another person with the gift of wisdom or discernment may need to temper that person's desire to help in certain circumstances. Sometimes the "merciful" person can become an enabler.

People with this gift often serve in ministries such as hospital and home visits, feeding the homeless, prison visitation, providing of meals, and other ministries that help those in need.

Word of Wisdom (*logos*: NT: 3056 something said including the thought); by implication a topic (subject of discourse), also reasoning (the mental faculty) or motive. *sophias*: NT:4678 from NT:4680; wisdom (higher or lower, worldly or spiritual): NT:4679; to render wise; in a sinister acceptation, to form "sophisms", i.e. continue plausible error. [12]

The Old Testament ideas about wisdom are embodied in people such as Joseph and Solomon. Both had a God-given ability to combine knowledge and experience and apply that to life's situations. Then of course we look to Jesus as the ultimate example of wisdom. We first hear of about the wisdom of Jesus in Luke 2:40: *"And the child grew and became strong; he was filled with wisdom, and the grace of God was upon him"* (NIV) and Luke 2:52: *"And Jesus grew in wisdom and stature, and in favor with God and men."* (NIV).

We see many instances of Jesus using His wisdom to teach, correct, and even rebuke when necessary. He, in fact, validated the wisdom of Solomon, but let the Pharisees know that He was greater than Solomon (Lk 11:31-32). In Luke 21:15, Jesus told His disciples He would give wisdom (sophia) so powerful that those who opposed them would not be able to resist or refute them. Remember that in Acts 3 those who were chosen to be deacons needed to have this wisdom. Stephen, who was one of those chosen as a deacon, proved this to be true in Acts 6:8-10: *"And Stephen, full of grace and power, was performing great wonders and signs among the people. But some men from what was called the Synagogue of the Freedmen, including both Cyrenians and Alexandrians, and some from Cilicia and Asia, rose up and argued with Stephen. But they were unable to cope with the wisdom and the Spirit with which he was speaking."*

Here again, we see that it is a supernatural ability. It was because of God given "grace and power" that Stephen could perform the signs and wonders he did and then speak with irrefutable wisdom. Now we know that he, along with the others in the early church, were devoting themselves to teaching, fellowship, prayer, and communion. This helped prepare Stephen to be used. Ultimately though, all of those whom God uses must rely on the power of the Spirit to bring wisdom to a specific situation. When we apply God's wisdom, the wisdom of the world has no chance.

1 Cor 1:19-25: *"For it is written: "I will destroy the wisdom of the wise; the intelligence of the intelligent I will frustrate." Where is the wise man? Where is the scholar? Where is the philosopher of this age? Has not God made foolish the wisdom of the world? For since in the wisdom of God the world through its wisdom did not know him, God was pleased through the foolishness of what was preached to save those who believe. Jews demand miraculous signs and Greeks look for wisdom, but we preach Christ crucified: a stumbling block to Jews and foolishness to Gentiles, but to those whom God has called, both Jews and Greeks, Christ the power of God and the wisdom of God. For the foolishness of God is wiser than man's wisdom, and the weakness of God is stronger than man's strength"* (NIV).

Rom 11:33-36: *"Oh, the depth of the riches of the wisdom and knowledge of God! How unsearchable his judgments, and his paths beyond tracing out! "Who has known the mind of the Lord? Or who has been his counselor?" "Who has ever given to God, that God should repay him?" For from him and through him and to him are all things. To him be the glory forever! Amen"* (NIV).

Use in the Church Today

We should realize first, that wisdom is promised to all believers who seek it from God. Consider the words of James 1:5-: *"If any of you lacks wisdom, he should ask God, who gives generously to all without finding fault, and it will be given to him. But when he asks, he must believe and not doubt, because he who doubts is like a wave of the sea, blown and tossed by the wind. That man should not think he will receive anything from the Lord; he is a double-minded man, unstable in all he does"* (NIV). We should not be afraid to ask for that supernatural wisdom ourselves, yet we are told that there are people who are supernaturally gifted in this area in order to build up the church.

James helps us to recognize this type of wisdom. Look at James 3:13 *"Who is wise and understanding among you? Let him show it by his good life, by deeds done in the humility that comes from wisdom."* Also, James 3:17-18: *"But the wisdom that comes from heaven is first of all pure; then peace-loving, considerate, submissive, full of mercy and good fruit, impartial and sincere. Peacemakers who sow in peace raise a harvest of righteousness"* (NIV).

This gift is especially helpful for those who would minister in areas such as counseling, prayer, and leadership, but of course is beneficial in just about every ministry to the body of Christ.

Word of Knowledge (logos again but coupled with *gnosis*: knowing, knowledge) This word is a little scary to work with. There was a group of people who claimed to be Christians but were called Gnostics (from *gnosis*) because they claimed to have "secret knowledge." The early church did not see the word in that sense, but in the sense that knowledge came from God. Knowledge could be found in the Old Testament scriptures but also in the teaching of Jesus and the apostles. Kittle says that *gnosis* can mean, "to detect," "to recognize," "to note," "to learn," or even "to confirm."

This is why we see the word of knowledge in basically two ways. One way is to have an understanding of God's Word that is especially keen on insight provided by the Holy Spirit. The other is to have a completely supernatural message or insight from God, something you could not know or learn, except the Spirit reveals it.

We see this operating in Jesus. He had insight into the Old Testament scriptures that no one else had. Matthew 7:28-29 says, *"When Jesus had finished saying these things, the crowds were amazed at his teaching, because he taught as one who had authority, and not as their teachers of the law"* (NIV). Jesus would explain the true meaning of the Jewish Scriptures because he had perfect knowledge. In the Sermon on the Mount, He used the expression, *"you have heard it said...but I tell you,"* showing that His knowledge was far beyond the knowledge of the rabbis. It was directly from God.

We also see the other form of *gnosis* demonstrated when Jesus dealt with different individuals. Remember the Samaritan woman at the well? *"He told her, 'Go, call your husband and come back.' 'I have no husband," she replied'. Jesus said to her, 'You are right when you say you have no husband. The fact is, you have had five husbands, and the man you now have is not your husband. What you have just said is quite true.' 'Sir,' the woman said, 'I can see that you are a prophet.'* (John 4:16-20). Then in Matthew 9:4 we read this: *"Knowing their thoughts, Jesus said, "Why do you entertain evil thoughts in your hearts?"* (NIV). (Also see Mk 2:8.)

Some may say, "yes, but that was Jesus and He knew everything because He was God." True, but the Bible teaches that some of His attributes were veiled so that Jesus could also be fully man (Phil 2:1).

I believe that in Jesus' humanity, He walked in perfect communion with the Father and the Holy Spirit and that is why He had perfect knowledge.

We also have examples of this gift operating in people in the book of Acts. Peter, who was not exactly a biblical scholar, was able to explain the Scriptures in a way that caused people to listen and they came to Christ in droves. One of the best examples of the second form of words of knowledge is when Ananias and Sapphira lied about their giving. The Holy Spirit revealed this lie to Peter and also that they would die for this sin.

Paul exercised this gift many times. Acts 13:9-11 says, *"Then Saul, who was also called Paul, filled with the Holy Spirit, looked straight at Elymas and said, 'You are a child of the devil and an enemy of everything that is right! You are full of all kinds of deceit and trickery. Will you never stop perverting the right ways of the Lord? Now the hand of the Lord is against you. You are going to be blind, and for a time you will be unable to see the light of the sun'* (NIV). In Acts 27 the ship that Paul was sailing on was caught in a violent storm. It was so bad that Luke states they had lost all hope of survival. Let's look at the account in Acts 27:21-25: *"After the men had gone a long time without food, Paul stood up before them and said: 'Men, you should have taken my advice not to sail from Crete; then you would have spared yourselves this damage and loss. But now I urge you to keep up your courage, because not one of you will be lost; only the ship will be destroyed. Last night an angel of the God whose I am and whom I serve stood beside me and said, 'Do not be afraid, Paul. You must stand trial before Caesar; and God has graciously given you the lives of all who sail with you.' So keep up your courage, men, for I have faith in God that it will happen just as he told me"* (NIV). In this case it was an angel that delivered the word of knowledge but it is still an example of God delivering a word supernaturally to be helpful in a given circumstance.

Use in the Church Today

There are many uses of word of knowledge today. Obviously a Bible teacher needs the first form of this gift. When it operates in a teacher, the body benefits in their understanding of God's Word. The first form of the gift is also invaluable in counseling. To be able to share biblical knowledge in a divinely inspired way can be a tremendous help to people who are going through tough times.

The second application of this gift is also extremely helpful in several areas. In counseling situations, sometimes a word of knowledge from God is necessary to break through a conflict where the truth may not be coming out.

In leading a church, sometimes the only way a good decision can be made is when God gives that special revelation in how to proceed. In individual ministries, God can provide needed direction with a word of knowledge. Even in the leadership of the home, a word of knowledge can be necessary for good decisions and God is able to provide that. You can see that this gift, when used in the proper way and at the proper time, can be a true blessing to the Church. When the Holy Spirit gives a word of knowledge and people can see that it is true and real, their faith in God's ability to intervene supernaturally in our lives is increased.

Faith (*pistis*: also translated belief, trust, assure, fidelity. Kittle states that in classical Greek, it could mean confidence, trust, trustworthiness, reliability, or assurance. Robertson says that the word here is not the same as your saving faith or faith of surrender but wonder working faith (1 Cor 13:2 or Mt 17:20; 20-21).

This gift of faith usually operates with other gifts such as miracles, healings, prophecies, or words of knowledge. Without faith, it is hard to actually use these other gifts. It would be difficult to tell someone who is paralyzed; "rise and walk" if you did not also have the faith that God would heal! It takes a supernatural faith to do that. We see it operating all throughout the ministry of Jesus and the apostles (Acts 3:16; 14:9).

But the gift of faith also operates in more subtle ways. Sometimes, the person with this gift will step out to do things that others will not do. The gift of faith shows up in obedience to God's leading, even when it may seem illogical or unreasonable. Stephen, whom the Bible says was "full of faith," was able to stand before the leaders of Israel and proclaim the Gospel, to face death by stoning, and to ask God not to hold their sin against them (Acts 7).

There are many accounts of obedience to God in tough circumstances, which could not have happened without a supernatural measure of faith in Him, but one great example is in Acts 21:10-14: *"As we were staying there for some days, a prophet named Agabus came down from Judea. And coming to us, he took Paul's belt and bound his own feet and hands, and said, 'This is what the Holy Spirit says: 'In this way the Jews at Jerusalem will bind the man who owns this belt and deliver him into the hands of the Gentiles.' When we had heard this, we as well as the local residents began begging him not to go up to Jerusalem. Then Paul answered, 'What are you doing, weeping and breaking my heart? For I am ready not only to be bound, but even to die at Jerusalem for the name of the Lord Jesus.' And since he would not be persuaded, we fell silent, remarking, 'The will of the Lord be done!'"* Paul was not questioning the prophecy, but exercising faith that no matter what God called him to, he would follow, even to his death.

Use in the Church Today

One of the great examples of this gift in operation in the church is the life of a man by the name of George Müller. Here is a short bio from Wikipedia:

The work of Müller and his wife with orphans began in 1836 with the preparation of their own rented home at 6 Wilson Street, Bristol for the accommodation of thirty girls. Soon after, three more houses in Wilson Street were furnished, not only for girls but also for boys and younger children, eventually increasing the capacity for children who could be cared for to 130.

In 1845, as growth continued, the neighbours complained about the noise and disruption to the public utilities, so Müller decided that a separate building designed to house 300 children was necessary, and in 1849, at Ashley Down, Bristol, that home opened. The architect commissioned to draw up the plans asked if he might do so gratuitously. By 26 May 1870, 1,722 children were being accommodated in five homes, although there was room for 2,050 (No 1 House – 300, No 2 House – 400, Nos 3, 4 and 5 – 450 each). By the following year, there were 280 orphans in No 1 House, 356 in No 2, 450 in Nos 3 and 4, and 309 in No 5 House.

Through all this, Müller never made requests for financial support, nor did he go into debt, even though the five homes cost over £100,000 to build. Many times, he received unsolicited food donations only hours before they were needed to feed the children, further strengthening his faith in God. For example, on one well-documented occasion, they gave thanks for breakfast when all the children were sitting at the table, even though there was nothing to eat in the house. As they finished praying, the baker knocked on the door with sufficient fresh bread to feed everyone, and the milkman gave them plenty of fresh milk because his cart broke down in front of the orphanage. [13]

Müller believed God was the one orchestrating the work and had such faith in Him that he would not ask for funds. He trusted God would provide and God came through! This has to be a special gift. No one can "muster up" more faith. It comes from asking God for this gift. That is why Paul emphasizes that we should "earnestly seek" the gifts. Faith will work in conjunction with all the gifts so that they are efficient and meaningful.

Have you ever noticed that when you see someone using this gift, it increases your desire for faith? That of course does not mean everyone will always have the extraordinary amount of faith that Müller had and that is ok. God gives as He wills and we rejoice to see the gift operate in others, but let us all be seeking to see faith operating in us more than we ever have before, especially when He calls us to do something we think we could never do.

Discernment of Spirits (discernment from the root word *diakrino: to separate thoroughly, to distinguish, judicially to try; Spirits from the word pneumation: wind or breath, which was the term used for spirit in Greek. In their thinking, the pneuma is that which imparts life in the spiritual sense as opposed to the fleshly sense).* [14]

Kittle says this: "in a unique sense pneuma is used of a soul thoroughly roused by the Holy Spirit and wholly intent on divine things, yet destitute of distinct self-consciousness and clear understanding; [15]

The concept here is that this gift gives the ability to put something said or done to "trial" to see if it is of God or if it is from human thought or even from the realm of Satan. It is also needed to determine if a person is under demonic influence or possessed. Jesus demonstrates this in Matthew 16:21-23: "From that time on Jesus began to explain to his disciples that he must go to Jerusalem and suffer many things at the hands of the elders, chief priests and teachers of the law, and that he must be killed and on the third day be raised to life. Peter took him aside and began to rebuke him. 'Never, Lord!' he said. 'This shall never happen to you!' Jesus turned and said to Peter, 'Get behind me, Satan! You are a stumbling block to me; you do not have in mind the things of God, but the things of men' (NIV). In the Gospels, we see many times where Jesus recognized "unclean spirits," demonic words and deeds (Lk 4:33, 8:29, 9:42).

Peter, in combination with a word of knowledge, discerns that a plot by Ananais and Sapphira to fool the church leaders is actually from Satan. Acts 5:3 says, "Then Peter said, 'Ananias, how is it that Satan has so filled your heart that you have lied to the Holy Spirit...?'"(NIV).

Remember the event with Elymas that was mentioned earlier, when Paul was used to strike him with blindness? This is what he said: "You are a child of the devil and an enemy of everything that is right! You are full of all kinds of deceit and trickery. Will you never stop perverting the right ways of the Lord?" (Acts 13:10 NIV). Paul could obviously discern that Elymas was "posing" as a seeker, but his real interest was in opposing God.

Use in the Church Today

Discernment of spirits is a much-needed gift today. There are, just as Jesus said, many "wolves in sheep's clothing" who would lead the sheep astray. Jesus warned of this in Matthew 7:15 and Paul reiterated it in Acts 20:29-30 *"I know that after I leave, savage wolves will come in among you and will not spare the flock. even from your own number men will arise and distort the truth in order to draw away disciples after them" (NIV).*

Satan, the father of lies, seeks to destroy the church and tries to deceive believers the same way he did in the Garden of Eden. He will use half-truths and all-out lies in order to accomplish this. Paul tells Timothy that Satan will be effective in this. 1 Timothy 4:1-2 says, "The Spirit clearly says that in later times some will abandon the faith and follow deceiving spirits and things taught by demons. Such teachings come through hypocritical liars, whose consciences have been seared as with a hot iron" (NIV). This is why God gives this wonderful gift to many.

It certainly is supernatural because those who exercise it will often say that they are not be able to explain, even Scripturally, why they have a check in their spirit about something said or done; they simply know it is wrong. Often times, God will affirm that check using someone with the gift of teaching or wisdom, who can show Scripturally why they recognized a deceiving spirit.

It would seem that all Pastors/Teachers would have this gift, but unfortunately that is not always the case. I have seen some of the greatest teachers in the world be unable to discern whether a person is legitimate or a phony with their own agenda. That is why a healthy church needs others with the gift of discernment to come alongside in leadership. This gift would be helpful for just about any form of service to the body, but especially in leadership of various ministries such as men's and women's groups, small home groups, or anything where someone with their own agenda might try to work their way into positions of authority.

It is especially important to those who go into foreign mission fields where satanic opposition often comes with a frontal assault rather than the subtle approach he takes in western culture. Demon possession is much more common in third world countries than here, but that does not mean it cannot happen even in America. I can guarantee from personal experience that without this gift, a person could put themselves in harm's way. Thank God that He has blessed us with these supernatural gifts in order to build His church!

Helps (*antilempseis: relief, laying hold of, help*)

Helps is listed in the text of 1 Corinthians 12:28. In context, three of the four offices, which are mentioned in Ephesians 4, are listed first, then more gifts are mentioned, some of which are repeated from earlier in the chapter. I think that is a clue in how the gift of helps is to be viewed. There are those people who are not gifted to be leaders in the body, but they are to help the leaders. Traditionally, we have seen this as similar to the gift of serving. In both cases, these gifted, behind-the-scenes helpers assist those who are "up front" in many different ways.

Paul writes a letter to Philemon on behalf of such a person whose mane is Onesimus. This is what he says about him: "I appeal to you for my son Onesimus, who became my son while I was in chains. Formerly he was useless to you, but now he has become useful both to you and to me. I would have liked to keep him with me so that he could take your place in helping me while I am in chains for the gospel" (Phlm 1:10-13, NIV).

In Ephesians 6, we hear about Tychicus whom Paul calls a faithful servant. Paul sends him to the church to report on Paul's ministry and wellbeing. "You know that the household of Stephanas were the first converts in Achaia, and they have devoted themselves to the service of the saints"(1 Cor 16:15, NIV). What stands out in these examples is that we do not really know how all these people helped, but the important thing is that they DID help! They were not in it for the recognition, but simply desired to use their spiritual gift to serve the body.

Use in the Church Today

The gift of helps is needed in every area of ministry. "Helps" is characterized by a desire to help those in charge, being an assistant. It's demonstrated by the passing out of bulletins on a Sunday morning service or in setting up the coffee cart, washing the communion cups, cooking the burgers, doing the slides, you name it. You can tell the one who is exercising this gift because the person loves helping and does not want recognition. This individual prefers to stay in the background and simply help the job to get done.

The people with this gift are the ones who pick up others needing a ride. They mow the lawn for those who cannot do it. They help people who are moving to a new place. They see a need and take initiative to help. Aren't we all thankful for people with this gift?

Administration (kubernetes: to steer, pilotage. Used for the helmsman of a ship) This goes beyond the gift of leadership and refers to those who give direction to a specific body. The Latin word for government comes from this word, so it is a gift necessary to those who would be running the church. Remember in Acts 6 where the seven were chosen to wait tables? The idea that came to the twelve to do that is an example of this gift operating in them.

Some other examples:

Acts 8:14-15 *"Now when the apostles in Jerusalem heard that Samaria had received the word of God, they sent them Peter and John, who came down and prayed for them that they might receive the Holy Spirit."*

Acts 15:22: *"Then it seemed good to the apostles and the elders, with the whole church, to choose men from among them to send to Antioch with Paul and Barnabas."*

1 Tm 1:3-4 *"As I urged you upon my departure for Macedonia, remain on at Ephesus so that you may instruct certain men not to teach strange doctrines, nor to pay attention to myths and endless genealogies, which give rise to mere speculation rather than furthering the administration of God which is by faith."*

You can see how the Holy Spirit gave the inspiration for decision making. This provides Godly direction to the church.

Use in the Church Today

Oh how we need those with the gift of administration in the church today. We need people who have the God-given ability to direct and govern the church. It isn't necessarily the pastor/teacher, but it certainly can be. I believe the gift of wisdom must work in conjunction with this gift to provide guidance for day-to-day operation and long-term vision for the local church as well as keeping an eye on the spiritual health of that body.

Other Possibilities of Gifts

A question often asked is, "are these two lists exhaustive, or are there any other spiritual gifts operating in the church?" It is a very good question. Let me list a few other qualities that some people consider to be spiritual gifts and the scriptures associated with that premise.

1. Craftsmanship-- Ex 31:3-5: *"I have filled him with the Spirit of God in wisdom, in understanding, in knowledge, and in all kinds of craftsmanship, to make artistic designs for work in gold, in silver, and in bronze, and in the cutting of stones for settings, and in the carving of wood, that he may work in all kinds of craftsmanship."*
2. Hospitality-- 1 Pt 4:9-11: *"Offer hospitality to one another without grumbling. Each one should use whatever gift he has received to serve others, faithfully administering God's grace in its various forms. If anyone speaks, he should do it as one speaking the very words of God. If anyone serves, he should do it with the strength God provides, so that in all things God may be praised through Jesus Christ. To him be the glory and the power for ever and ever. Amen" (NIV).*
3. Intercession or intercessory prayer--Rom 8:26-27: *"In the same way the Spirit also helps our weakness; for we do not know how to pray as we should, but the Spirit Himself intercedes for us with groanings too deep for words; and He who searches the hearts knows what the mind of the Spirit is, because He intercedes for the saints according to the will of God" (NIV).*

   Col 4:12: *"Epaphras, who is one of your number, a bondslave of Jesus Christ, sends you his greetings, always laboring earnestly for you in his prayers" (NIV).*

I think you can make a case for these as gifts, but I would not put them in the same category as the ones listed by Paul. Certainly, in the example of craftsmanship, it was a work done by the power of the Spirit, but again not in the same sense as when we are filled with the Spirit as New Testament believers. With hospitality, it seems Peter is saying that all of us should offer hospitality and then he repeats a couple of the gifts listed by Paul. In the verses concerning intercession, nowhere does it mention it as a spiritual gift. I would not, however, take issue with those who see it as one of the gifts.

None of what I have just said should in any way take away from the value of the three qualities just listed. There are others that people mention as well. These are important abilities God is using in people's lives and they certainly can be used to edify the body, which is the main purpose of spiritual gifts. I suggest we not become too picky on whether or not these qualify as "spiritual gifts." I just like to stick to the ones that are specifically listed as such. I might also suggest that even if you feel that one of these may be your main gift, that you seek others as well. We don't want to fall short of anything that God desires for us!

Discovering Your Gifts

In any discussion of spiritual gifts, the question most often asked is, "how do I know what my gifts are?" Usually those who ask that fear they do not have any gift or gifts. The underlying thought may be, "of course I don't have any gifts because I am not worthy to be used by God" or "I am not spiritual enough for God to give me any gifts." The good news is that gifts are not based on our worthiness but on God's grace. Remember, at the very beginning of the book we stated that the word for spiritual gift is a word used for grace.

You must realize that God has given you a gift or gifts and consider that if you are not exercising your gift/gifts, the body is actually being deprived. Your gift/gifts are just as important to the body as anyone's. Corinthians 12:14-16 says, *"For the body is not one member, but many. If the foot says, "Because I am not a hand, I am not a part of the body," it is not for this reason any the less a part of the body. And if the ear says, 'Because I am not an eye, I am not a part of the body,' it is not for this reason any the less a part of the body." The answer of course is no! So take the time to evaluate what gift or gifts God has given you, so that you can bless the rest of the body.*

When seeking to find out what gifts you have, there are important things to consider and important actions to take.

1. Examine your life and your walk with Jesus. "If we live by the Spirit, let us also walk by the Spirit" (Gal 5:25-26). Determine whether you have truly surrendered your heart to the Lord and control of your life to the Holy Spirit. Even though your gifts are by His grace, the more you walk by His Spirit, the more He will use those gifts.
2. Ask God to reveal to you what your gifts are and to lead you to ministries that will benefit from them. That may mean to start by serving in several different capacities, filling needs that arise. When you do this, ask yourself these questions:

   a. *Do I enjoy this? Does it seem like an obligation or do I love doing it?*
   b. *Do I see fruit coming from this?*

   c. *Do others recognize an ability in me that helps make this ministry successful?*

4. Take a spiritual gifts inventory. There are good resources available that can help you to come to conclusions of where your gifts lie. This should be used along with the above mentioned, not singularly. Though the people who do these inventories have spent much time in matching the questions with biblical teaching, the tests are still man-made and therefore not perfect.

Always keep in mind that it is God who gives the gifts. We are just being obedient to His calling when we use them to edify the church. Give Him the glory for the blessings that come from your obedience. Continue to seek earnestly other gifts, but don't be envious of others that may have gifts you would like to have. If it is not God's plan for you to have that gift, He has a good and perfect reason. Rejoice in the gifts He has bestowed upon you and use them to the fullest!

About The Author

Kris Van Hook serves as an Assistant Pastor at Living Truth Christian Fellowship in Corona, CA. Prior to coming on staff full-time, he taught physical education and health at Garden Grove High School. He was a high school teacher and coach for thirty seven years. During that time he helped establish Calvary Chapel High School, where he served as Assistant Principal, Athletic Director and Head Football Coach. He has also served in several other Calvary Chapel church ministries. His first call to ministry was as a Youth Pastor at First Baptist Church in Fullerton, Ca. Kris is married to wife Shawn and has three grown children and nine grandchildren.

Email: coachkvh@gmail.com

To listen to any of Pastor Kris' messages as well as those from any of the other Pastors at LTCF, visit www.livingtruthcorona.org and go to "sermons."

Endnotes

1. Strong, James. *Biblesoft's New Exhaustive Strong's Numbers and Concordance with Expanded Greek-Hebrew Dictionary.* Walter, et al., The Bible Knowledge Commentary (Old Testament). Colorado Springs: Cook Communications, 2000.

2. Barnes' Notes, Electronic Database 2006 by Biblesoft, Inc.

3. Theological Dictionary of the New Testament.

4. Kenneth Kitchen, "On the Reliability of the Old Testament" (Eerdman's, 2003), pp.261-263

5. from www.churchleaders.com *7 Startling Facts: An Up Close Look at Church Attendance in America* 11/4/14

6. Strong, James. *Biblesoft's New Exhaustive Strong's Numbers and Concordance with Expanded Greek-Hebrew Dictionary.* Walter, et al., The Bible Knowledge Commentary (Old Testament). Colorado Springs: Cook Communications, 2000.

7. Theological Dictionary of the New Testament   1972-1989 By Wm. B. Eerdmans Publishing Co. 1989

8. Biblesoft's New Exhaustive Strong's Numbers and Concordance with Expanded Greek-Hebrew Dictionary. 2000

9. Biblesoft's New Exhaustive Strong's Numbers and Concordance with Expanded Greek-Hebrew Dictionary. 2000

10. Biblesoft's New Exhaustive Strong's Numbers and Concordance with Expanded Greek-Hebrew Dictionary. 2000

11. Biblesoft's New Exhaustive Strong's Numbers and Concordance with Expanded Greek-Hebrew Dictionary. 2000

12. Biblesoft's New Exhaustive Strong's Numbers and Concordance with Expanded Greek-Hebrew Dictionary. 2000

13. http://en.wikipedia.org/wiki/George_Müller 11/4/14

14. Biblesoft's New Exhaustive Strong's Numbers and Concordance with Expanded Greek-Hebrew Dictionary. 2000

15. Theological Dictionary of the New Testament   1972-1989 By Wm. B. Eerdmans Publishing Co. 1989

Made in the USA
Las Vegas, NV
01 July 2021

25770901R00046